MICRO - ENTREPRENEURSHIP

A Simple Guide of Ideas to Create a Proactive Attitude and Mindset to Start: A Business of Your Own to Have a Life That You Want to Live

A Key to Living the Life of Happiness with more Wealth

RAM YAKSH

ISBN 979-8-89322-673-7

The book titled **"MICRO-ENTERPRENEURSHIP"** is about the social -
Economic problem being faced worldwide related to unemployment.
The author has very well connected the life cycle experience and has
given some innovative suggestions to overcome this problem.

As per old Indian culture majorities of the families used their family
skills from generation to generation for their earnings.However the
shift in this approach has taken place gradually with the advancement
of science and lucrative city life.The suggestions given in the book
revolves around this old Indian philosophy.

In my opinion the implementation and adoption of this system
in present national and international environment may not be easy
as benefits can only be realised on long term basis.In order to make
this concept adoptable lot of efforts are required .The author has also
suggested improvement / measures to be taken by individual,society
and by government both at national and international levels.

Mr Ram Nath Yaksh ,with his rich experience and relevent
educational background has identified the future areas of growth
and concluded by emphasising the need of change in the mind set to
business over job

Devendra Raina
Ex Executive Director
Bharat Heavy Electricals Ltd
New Delhi India

The book authored by Mr RamYaksh, a Canada based entrepreneur with vast experience of Indian and global markets is a must read reference handbook for all budding microentrepreneurs.

It covers the five Ws and H of micro entrepreneurship i.e. What is the concept, Who all should enter the field, Why the adoption of the concept is necessary, Where all lies the scope of Micro Entrepreneurship, When all a budding entrepreneur in all age groups and strata of society can generate ideas and how they are to be put into action. The language of the book is simple and easily understandable.

The core idea of the book is Increasing earning capacity thereby increasing purchasing power.

Author aims to invoke a thought process for using practical knowledge to incubate ideas to acquire a business mindset thus initiating entrepreneurship .

The book touches upon the current inflation, taxation scenario across the globe necessitating micro entrepreneurship and its possibilities in both rural and urban areas.

The most important part of the book is self introspection and investigating questions for every budding entrepreneur.

The book also has suggestions and possibilities for all those who are ready to take an entrepreneurial plunge globally. It also has recommendations for Government institutions to promote the culture of microentrepreneurship.

This book should be a part of all institutions imparting formal education , dealing with policy formulation and implementation of this concept. This book needs to be translated into regional languages as well for broader reach of the society.

Col Tarun Chhibber, Veteran

Regiment of Artillery

Superannuation 2016

Settled in Panchkula,

Haryana,

India

Dear sir,

The book "Micro-entrepreneurship, written by author Ram Yaksh speaks of possibility of entrepreneurship, by groups of all ages and financial status,irrespective of educational levels. It provides excellent and precious ideas to kickstart startups in a simple language. This book is the need of hour which aims to increase the earning capacity to increase the purchasing power. This is a must read book.

Dr. Dinesh Rana,
Dy. Medical Superintendent,
LLRM Medical College, Meerut, UP.

Contents

Acknowledgements 9

Introduction 11

Significance of Micro-entrepreneurship 13

The Journey from Entrepreneurship to Industrialist 17

Inflation and Its Impact 18

Micro-entrepreneurship 19

Tax Structure and Taxation 21

Part I Introspection and Workshop **23**

The Thought Process of People, Businessmen, and Government 25

Mindsets of Salaried, Self-employed, and Business People 26

Micro-entrepreneurship Possibilities in Rural Areas 28

Micro-entrepreneurship in Urban Areas 31

Governmental Efforts and Support System 33

Business Mindset Questions to be Asked Before Starting Business 36

Contribution of Press, the IVth Estate 38

Part II Introspection and Workshop **39**

Mentorship and Quality Control 41

Human Resource Development Support System 42

Banking and Accounting Support 43

Product Placement Questions and Information to Be Gathered 45

Product R&D and Testing 46

Cost Reduction Measures 48

Idea to business conversion 49

Part III Introspection and Workshop **53**

Education System and Changes Required 55

Change of Mindset Through Education 58

Long-term Impact of Entrepreneurship 59

Short-term Impact of Entrepreneurship 62

Recycling of Waste 63

Business in the Financial Sector 65

Common Home-based Business 66

Part IV Introspection and Workshop **69**

Conclusion 71

Acknowledgements

I express my gratitude to my children for listening to the concept of this book. They agreed with me that a book on this topic is badly needed, especially when most people are finding it difficult to run their houses because of limited income and ever-increasing expenses due to inflation. They probably feel that a common person like them cannot start a business easily without the burden and heavy baggage of expenses and loans. Why are people hesitant to start their own business confidently and prefer to stick to their jobs initially until the business picks up substantially?

The reason probably lies in the fact that the teachers who taught us were doing a job themselves, so they could give us the mindset of a job but not the mindset of a business person. This is more of a mindset problem than anything else.

I dedicate this book to my late grandparents and parents, who ignited humanity in me and taught me community feelings, ethics, values, and philanthropy. I am grateful to my family for always standing like a rock with me, rendering all possible cooperation as and when needed. Not forgetting my daughter, who helped me a lot while I was writing this book. I would like to dedicate this book to my ancestors and my deep Indian Sanatan roots.

I am grateful to everyone who helped me as much as they could to make this book a possibility. They also believed that a business mindset is the need of the hour everywhere and in every country.

Ram Yaksh

Introduction

This book was written in the year 2023, when most of the world was reeling under inflation; many countries were standing at the doorstep of recession, while some countries with very heavy debt were close to bankruptcy. But the world is still moving on, with many layoffs and ever-reducing per capita purchasing power. The people are living paycheque to paycheque. It's never too late to take remedial measures, as there is always a dawn after the darkest night.

The world's largest economies—the United States, China, Japan, and the European Union—are suffering from inflation with a fear of going into recession. I strongly feel that we need to increase our purchasing power by increasing our earning capacity.

This book in your hand shows that you have a strong desire to start your own business.

I am sure you will find this book interesting and discover some thought-provoking ideas to have the mindset to start a business and succeed in it.

Significance of Micro-Entrepreneurship

This book will inspire many minds and governments of various countries to take effective measures to increase their per capita income by motivating people to start a business of their own. The business can contain some of the inflation or neutralise it by increasing per capita income significantly from grassroots levels, thereby improving the standard of living.

Let us increase our earning power by giving meaningful education to youths at grassroots levels. As we make all our efforts to get a job, let us, with strong passion and conviction, start our own business, even if it is small. Over a period of time, even the smallest business can grow, generating more income than a good job. When we can use academic knowledge to do a job, then why can't we use the same knowledge and ideas to kickstart small businesses to create wealth? Every human being has enough practical knowledge and ideas to start a business; all they need is a little courage, self-belief, and a business mindset.

The business environment around us provides us with many inputs, ideas, and practical knowledge. They give us insights on initiating and running our business successfully, which not only generates wealth but also employment.

I have worked more than 30 years in pharmaceuticals in different positions, and then I was involved in research on immunity-building products as a product executive. I have worked as a general sales manager in the pharma sector and even run my own pharmaceutical company and an advertising company. I have marketed weighbridges, industrial chemicals, and industrial engines.

For more than 15 years, I was a financial adviser in the financial sector. In my tenure as a financial adviser, I interacted with various banks, financial institutions, and insurance and mutual fund companies. I have the experience of being an employee, a self-employed individual, and an entrepreneur in different fields.

I have realised that I can save more tax as a businessman compared to a salaried employee by showing some expenses that are legally allowed as deductions. After all these experiences, I can conclude that business is the most profitable option because here we create a permanent source of income that will work for generations. We can multiply our income by hiring people to help us grow. While on our business journey, we will be exposed to many other businesses that will add to our knowledge and experience and provide us with insights that will be useful for our business. I grew more mentally and professionally while in business than in any other job. I also learnt practically that we pay more tax when in a job compared to business. All these prompted me to write this book.

We study for 15 years at least to complete our graduation but do not get a job of our liking, a workplace of our liking, or the salary we think we deserve. We are in perpetual fear of losing our jobs at any time.

Businesses take mostly three to five years to establish, but once settled, they are there for a lifetime and there is no fear of losing them. We can start our business part-time or full-time, depending on our situation. We can also start a part-time business while studying if we have the full backing of our family.

A businessperson goes through various stages in his journey to make a profitable business.

Stage I: We do the groundwork before initiating the business. In this stage, we connect with the community and try to understand the requirements that need to be fulfilled, which in turn will help the business that we will pursue. We learn from others' experiences, from their mistakes and successes. This not only provides information but also stretches our minds a little more.

As we gain more clarity, we become more focused and decide on the business that we want to do. We start working on putting our plans and learnings into action. Soon we will start believing in ideas and working towards making them work. This will increase our confidence to move on.

Stage II: As our business grows, we connect more to the needs of society around us, which interestingly becomes a creative field, giving us feedback almost daily in the form of customer complaints or satisfaction and operational setbacks.

Stage III: A business helps us grow both internally and externally. It builds resilience and keeps us on our toes. We learn a lot of things as a result of the all-round exposure that a business provides. We master interpersonal skills as our business grows. As we gain more experience and exposure to the journey of our business, finding solutions will come naturally to us. We will effortlessly turn our challenges into an advantage for our business.

Stage IV: This is an ongoing journey that keeps upgrading and fine-tuning us professionally. We learn to deal with different scenarios and the complexities that the future might throw at us. We become intensely practical, analytical, and professionally mature enough to make complex decisions, many times even for other businesses that interest us. Now we have a strong mindset, clarity, confidence, vision, self-belief, and passion to succeed, come what may. We have all that is needed to succeed. We also have a vision of our goals and the system we want to follow to achieve our vision and mission.

This is how many people who started from a small tea stall have expanded their business to several outlets. Some started out selling home-cooked food, grew to become office lunch suppliers, and expanded the business to a full-grown chain of restaurants. There is no specific age to start a business. A woman in India started a business at the age of 90 selling 'Besan Ki Barfi' and became a big brand. All she wanted was to earn money on her own. We are human beings, and each one of us has our own individual vibrations and energy. We are connected to the whole universe through God within us.

Once we start the business, services like accounting, logistics, or packing materials also take off. When we solve our own problems, we save time and get peace of mind. But when we solve the problem of the masses, then we gift a business opportunity to ourselves and jobs to many.

As a businessperson, we become a hero of our family. We are creating a source of permanent income for us and the coming generation. This thought keeps the family involved, happy, united, and prosperous with growing business.

It is so creative and exciting to create the future of our generations and, in the process, contribute to the economy of our nation as well. The process is a little challenging but greatly rewarding and fulfilling, which, in turn, makes us the masters of our own destiny. Doing business requires one to make a virtual shift in the mindset of the coming generation to grow the business to new heights.

The lives of 41 trapped workers were saved from a tunnel named Silk Yara, which had caved in and collapsed, in Operation Jeevan. That proved that humans, with their brains and innovations, are more powerful than artificial intelligence and the most powerful machines.

The art of doing business is nothing more than a mindset issue. Right from our childhood, the job mindset has been put in our minds by our teachers, parents, family, and friends, which takes time to shed.

We must be open to developing the business mindset that is primarily needed, while skillsets can always be learnt with a time-bound programme and planning. We can start with a small business, which is not difficult, and go on to become giant industrialists.

We are talking about AI (artificial intelligence) when not even 15% of the world is in business to create jobs. How is it possible to create 100% employment? Why don't we leverage human intelligence, precious time, and knowledge until he is alive to create micro-entrepreneurship? There is, therefore, a huge scope of business all over the world. Do we need AI at all?

The Journey from Entrepreneurship to Industrialist

When we start a business, we use locally available raw materials to save time, money, and energy. This saves money and also provides an opportunity for local businesses to grow. With such a thought process, when we connect with society, we grow our industrial mindset. This deepens our connection with society, gives us continuous feedback, and creates wealth. This addresses important local issues and, at times, national ones, which creates a better future for the whole nation.

There is a fine line that divides the businessman and the industrialist; a businessman works in the sectors that give maximum profit, while industrialists make a profit by solving community problems.

Industrialists have a better rapport with the community compared to businesspeople, as a result, they see opportunities in different fields depending on the needs of society. He also keeps getting continuous feedback about the product's performance and makes changes to ensure that the product satisfies the end user. This makes him competitive and competent at the same time. Entry into other sectors of the business becomes easier for him because of his close connection with society.

Inflation and Its Impact

Inflation occurs when the government, instead of encouraging more startups, prints more currency to cover up the deficit because the government has an ever-increasing need for money for growth in several sectors. With this continuing, ultimately the government will use the money in social schemes for people. The compounding impact of inflation continues, and many things become out of reach for a large portion of the population.

Thus, the industry decreases production as there is an artificial decrease in demand. This compels the companies to decrease production and, in turn, lay off some employees. This causes a decrease in employment. Now we have less production and less demand, but more unemployment. In fact, the economy has slid into a state of recession.

We must make all efforts to increase the earning capacity of the people. With little effort and investment from savings, people could be encouraged to start a business or micro-entrepreneurship and lead a comfortable life. We need to make predictable changes in our banking and education system and, if need be, make visible changes in existing laws to encourage a business mindset right from the beginning.

The current education system does not relate to market demand. Anywhere in the world, there is no system to predict the number of technicians, scientists, doctors, engineers, teachers, and construction workers needed every year. This makes micro-entrepreneurship so relevant and necessary because most of these people can productively utilise their knowledge and skills in businesses of their own.

Micro-Entrepreneurship

We should allow the applicable skills of the poorest of the poor to be used and translate those skills into a source of regular income by facilitating business at a micro level. For example, a person with knowledge of confectionery can start making biscuits, rusks, bread, etc., and sell them. They can keep upgrading their product list from time to time, depending on demand. Locally available raw materials can be used to cause inclusive growth at the micro level. Micro-entrepreneurship also ensures the productive use of knowledge, which is the most precious human resource.

Similarly, in urban areas, a few IT professionals, lawyers, construction workers, and coaches of different sports can start their own small companies. They can provide support to small farms, nearby schools and institutions, and businesses. This will give them business and create some employment opportunities. They can transform themselves from job takers to job givers.

The students should be encouraged to visit business houses to discuss with the owners how they started. It will give them in-depth clarity, hope, courage, and the mindset to start the business. Throughout our journey of starting and running a business, we keep learning from the business environments around us. This helps us master our business and gives us the confidence to expand it.

God has not made even one dust particle without any purpose. The vegetable, plant, and biomass waste can be converted into fertiliser; the glass, plastic, paper waste, and metal waste can be recycled, so why can't knowledge, the most precious resource of a human being, be utilised to create wealth till his last breath? When we can use a man's organs after death, then why can't we use his knowledge while he is alive? That belief can make him useful to society throughout his life. This book has been written with that principle and intention in mind.

Tax Structure and Taxation

Income tax on salaried people is increasing the world over. In addition, they pay tax in the form of GST on the products they buy for their daily needs. This reduces savings for emergencies by reducing net carry-home income. This puts many things beyond the reach of the salaried class.

Businesspeople have the option to save taxes by showing expenses and getting deductions, which the salaried class legally can't do. Business people can save taxes in two ways: first, by getting a benefit by showing expenses as business expenditures, and second, by paying less income tax. Following are the lowest and the highest income tax rates in some of the countries:

Country	Salaried individual	Corporations
India	5% to 30%	15% to 22%
USA	10% (federal) + 0–3.07% (state) + 0–3.8398% (local) (federal standard deduction of 12550 USD for single taxpayers)	Flat 21%
Japan	15.105% (5.105% national + 10% local)	29.74%

Source: https://en.wikipedia.org/wiki/List_of_countries_by_tax_rates

The businessman ends up paying lesser taxes when the government gives certain tax incentives to increase production and jobs and boost exports as they have huge turnover.

Size of some of the big economies and their GDP:

Rank & Country	GDP (USD billion)	GDP Per Capita (USD thousand)
#1 United States Of America (USA)	27,974	83.06
#2 China	18,566	13.16
#3 Germany	4,730	56.04
#4 Japan	4,291	34.55
#5 India	4,112	2.85
#6 United Kingdom (U.K.)	3,592	52.43
#7 France	3,182	48.22
#8 Italy	2,280	38.93
#9 Brazil	2,272	11.03
#10 Canada	2,242	55.53

Source: https://www.forbesindia.com/article/explainers/top-10-largest-economies-in-the-world/86159/1#:~:text=The%20United%20States%20of,magnitude%20of%20a%20nation's%20economy.

Part I

Introspection and Workshop

- Do you know that even small businesses can provide a better income than a good job?

- Everybody, irrespective of qualification or age, has some ideas about starting a business of their own. What are your ideas? Be passionate and give them shape.

- Which business have you decided to start?

- Do you want to be a businessman or an industrialist?

- Business people pay less income tax than those doing a job.

- Micro-entrepreneurship or startup allows us to become job providers.

- Business gives practical learning. You learn and grow along the way.

- It takes a minimum of five years to establish a business.

The Thought Process of People, Businessmen, and Government

What people think: The government must give jobs to all the people.

What the government thinks: The creation of revenue is a must for activities, such as public amenities, the banking system, and the maintenance of the army and police. Job creation is done by businessmen as well; they increase the number of taxpayers and increase government revenue collection. Perhaps this is the reason why businessmen can pay their taxes at reduced rates. If there is a shortage of revenue, it is better to print more currency.

What businesspeople think: We have done business with a lot of effort and investment. We are already creating jobs and paying taxes as well.

Mindsets of Salaried, Self-Employed, and Business People

A salaried person thinks he does not have any burden as he must do his duty from nine to five and then return home. In fact, he carries the most worries and tension. The salary on the salary sheet may look attractive, but what he takes home after tax is much less. The impact of inflation and the tax paid on all the household things he buys every month hardly leaves any savings for an emergency. He has no option but to live paycheck-to-paycheck. He does not visualise how much money he will need when he will not be able to work any longer. He can't make provision for that.

A self-employed person thinks he's a businessman. He spends long hours at work to earn more money. He forgets that he has employed himself on a job and carries very high risk with the benefits of being employed.

Self-employed and employed professionals have short-term solutions for the permanent need for income.

The difference between a businessman and an employed person:

- A businessman owns his business for generations, but the one who is in a job does not own that job permanently, even for himself. He can be shown a pink slip at any time.

- Those in business multiply their hours to create a permanent source of income to fulfil their dreams, but those in a job work for the dreams of their employer.

- A businessman connects with society and makes his own place in it as a businessman.

- A businessman creates jobs for others, but the one who is doing a job only works hard to remain in that job.

  The businessperson becomes a hero of his family; his children don't have to run after getting jobs. He can always increase his income. However, the person in a job has limited income and retires after a certain age with no significant savings. His children also search for jobs when they grow up. The businessman motivates and guides his children to do business and be with him. While the person in a job must be prepared to send his children out for a job and many times out of state, even out of the country.

Actual difference between the self-employed and those who are in a job:

- The self-employed person always carries the illusion that he is doing business, but he has taken a heavy risk of investment to employ himself. But the one who is doing a job does not have that risk.

- The self-employed is not sure that his coming generation will even carry forward or do what he is doing.

- He is always tensed that if anything happens to him, the whole so-called business is gone, just as in the case of an employed person. Who will look after the family? Both are unable to motivate the children to follow them.

Micro-Entrepreneurship Possibilities in Rural Areas

- Conversion of knowledge into wealth by making pickles, jams, rusks, biscuits, bread, and instant noodles, or production of ketchup from freshly picked tomatoes and chips from potatoes.

- Forward integration of wheat, black gram, bajra, and other agricultural produce. Forward integration means selling products directly to customers by bypassing middlemen to increase profitability and market share. They can involve youth who are pursuing marketing as their career. This will provide them with a sort of internship in marketing and maturity for business. Products such as homemade pickles, jam, ketchup, etc., can also be sold in this manner.

- Making different varieties of dry salted snacks.

- Creation of rural food outlets on a cooperative basis; creation of cooperatives to install machines to take out pulses, wheat, and rice from their respective crops and give higher prices to the growers of these crops.

- Formation of oil-extracting cooperatives in villages to extract oil from coconut, peanuts, mustard seeds, and sesame seeds, giving better prices to the farmers and good products to end users.

- The government must start technical institutes in villages to facilitate technical education for rural children. This will help them create and invent cost-effective agricultural machinery.

- Rainwater harvesting will help in the conservation and storage of water for irrigation and raise the water level of the ground. This will also save the cost of irrigation.

- Freshwater pearl harvesting and growing mushrooms and trees for paper pulp can be a good source of income. Electricity can be generated by constructing small windmills and through solar power.

- Energy can be generated from biomass, crop waste, dried leaves, and waste. Infertile land can be reclaimed by using vegetable waste, crop waste, and biowaste fertiliser, making it suitable for farming. Collective farming can reduce costs and increase production, leading to more income.

- Making cardboard, disposable biodegradable plates, and packing paper from crop waste can generate employment and is a good business option for people in rural areas. Sugarcane fibre can also be used to make cardboard boxes and paper. They are already doing this in Mauritius. They can also make ethanol from sugarcane bagasse and post-crop harvesting waste.

- A mill can be set up to make starch from corn, potatoes, and cassava, and flour from chickpea crops, corn, millet, wheat, and other food grains.

- Beekeeping is another business idea that doesn't require technical knowledge or a big investment.

- People who are passionate about plants can grow herbs and flowers commercially.

- Business can be created by making an emporium showcasing village life along with food courts to encourage rural tourism, which can cause a significant increase in the income of people in that area.

All the above activities can create a host of jobs in rural areas and make them self-sufficient. This will also help the rural children gain technical knowledge, which in turn will help them generate income.

One of the biggest problems in rural areas is that most of the farmers, irrespective of their affordability, want to own tractors, harvesting machines, and other equipment needed for farming. This increases their fixed costs individually. If they switch over to collective farming, they need not buy their own equipment, which can save them the maintenance cost of the equipment. This will also help them when they buy seeds and fertilisers by giving them bargaining power and economy of scale. Not only this, but the foundation will be laid for the future manufacturing of finished products from their agricultural produce. There can be innovation for moringa leaves/beans, black-eyed peas, soya beans, horse gram, millets, and Turkish gram-based products, which are of high nutritional value. Not much research has been done on these crops. Through innovation and research, multiple products with high nutritional value can be produced to increase the income of farmers. They can also provide snacks with high nutritional value to the consumers. There can be profit-sharing-based PSUs or farmers' cooperatives to give a boost to their income.

Similarly, sugar cane is another crop which is highly profitable for the sugar industry but is not of much profit for the farmers. In this sector also there can be PSUs or farmers cooperatives on profit sharing basis. The sugar cane industry makes more than 20 byproducts of sugarcane. We need to think and act on it. These measures can also make farming a field of great profit. In India, Amul Dairy is a living and vibrant example of a successful cooperative.

More than 25% of fruits and vegetables and a huge percentage of food grains are lost or destroyed in transit. Forward integration in these areas will not only give more value to the produce but also prevent huge losses. This applies to all the countries with agricultural produce.

Forward integration of agricultural produce and the formation of cooperatives will make agriculture one of the most profitable businesses and will play a dominant role in bringing down poverty drastically. This will lift even the smallest farmer above the poverty line. The farmers will be able to come out of their debt trap. Various measures are suggested to increase and maintain the area of agricultural land for the ever-increasing need for food grains, fruits and vegetables, and pulses all over the world. This should be given top priority by any nation to grow fast and reduce expenditure on health and infrastructure.

Micro-Entrepreneurship in Urban Areas

- Small IT companies can be started with unemployed IT professionals as well as IT students to support schools, small businesses, restaurants, recreation places, shops, and clubs.

- Small accounting companies can be started to provide auditing support to small companies, schools, colleges, shops, and other small businesses.

- Small service cooperatives or companies can be formed to provide services like electrical, plumbing, marbling, sanitary, house construction, carpentry, and painting services. This will employ the urban population and connect them to the customers.

- Providing authentic home-cooked food to office goers at affordable prices. This will make women financially independent by providing them with an opportunity to earn money in their spare time. Opening consumer cooperative stores will provide household consumables at affordable rates to people at reasonable prices, as well as create employment.

- Encouraging kitchen gardens; the kitchen gardens will provide fresh vegetables and fruits, and the extra production can be sold in cooperatives to generate extra income for the people who grow them.

- People with vehicles and the skill to drive can provide transport facilities at small distances like railway stations, schools, bus depots, and for festival occasions with their own travel or transport companies. They can also provide wholesale shopping services for the urban cooperatives from nearby villages.

- Coaching centres can be created by groups of children pursuing higher studies for children in junior classes for coaching purposes. This will provide them with pocket money, and they will be able to support their studies financially.

These are some of the ideas where they can use the knowledge to start a business.

Many of the above businesses can be done from anywhere, irrespective of geography, keeping the rules, regulations, and licence requirements in mind.

Governmental Efforts and Support System

- The government should help support the creation and identification of natural preservatives for products and perishables to prevent adverse effects on health caused by artificial preservatives.

- Facilitate the collaboration of entrepreneurs to further innovate, diversify, and enhance their businesses.

- Facilitate online and offline sales of products in the customer markets.

- Acquaint yourself with business people to find and reach the market.

- Provide banking help and communication from similar industries/ marketing experts to help make the products marketable.

- Organise visits by delegations of experts from other states and overseas to educate businessmen on the latest trends and the future course of growth in that particular industry. This can boost exports.

- Provide know-how to minimise waste and maximise productivity.

- The government can provide facilities for young entrepreneurs to supply food and fruits in train and air travel in collaboration with the government. The governmental establishment, local schools, and universities must buy their requirements from local entrepreneurs. This will reduce the cost of the product, save on transportation expenses and provide crucial support to upcoming local entrepreneurs.

- The government, with the help of local people and businessmen, can connect the urban areas with the nearest rural areas and vice versa. Such a move helps the rural businessman reach the customer faster. The government can also connect the remotest, inaccessible areas with the nearest town/district. This will create opportunities for business activities to take place and make the area prosperous.

- The government should also create a separate department for senior citizens' skill utilisation in the Ministry of Skill Development, wherein they can use their skills and knowledge to guide people. This will generate income for them, and they will be self-sufficient.

- The government needs to support research in the field of agriculture with the help of agriculture scientists, biotechnologists, and soil scientists to create human-friendly and safe natural pesticides and fertilisers and technology to increase agricultural crop production per hectare. This will not only make agriculture more profitable but will also help prevent various diseases that are caused by lack of nutrition.

- Depending on the product or service of the entrepreneur, the government should give holidays from GST, corporate tax, and income tax for five to ten years. This will help the startup become profitable quickly.

- Women must be trained to use their skills to generate income. When we empower a woman, we empower a family, and through one family, we empower the entire nation. We also minimise crimes against women. When they become financially independent, they contribute to the overall income of the family. They are more social, communicate better than men, and are more empathetic. In cases of adversity or her husband's death, she can manage on her own. There are live examples of many women the world over who started small businesses and converted them into big family empires. Thus, the financial empowerment of women can take a nation's economy to the next level.

- There should be one point of registration to start any business, where one can register their business with all relevant data. It will be better if information about the business is also made available.

- The government should make changes to the laws to allow certain businesses to be conducted from home without compromising on safety factors. We should remember that before the East India Company came to Bharat, there were small traditional family businesses all over. This is the reason India was called the golden bird. There are several retired or handicapped professionals, such as doctors, engineers, scientists, educationists established players, lawyers, army officers, etc., who carry great practical knowledge that can be useful for the nation and create wealth. The government should create a database, connect them online with startups, and use their services in exchange for a fee or payment. Such connectivity and use of knowledge can make a huge contribution to the economy of any nation. Such experiments can also be done for gifted children as well as women in rural and urban areas, where they can use their knowledge to start their own startups. Let everybody's knowledge, time, and skills be leveraged part-time/whole time to create wealth.

- After a discussion with some insurance companies, the government can introduce Startup Capital Insurance to help increase the startup's success rate. The premium should be a one-time payment for a five-year term. Part of the premium, about 25% to 50%, is to be shared by the government. This will increase the success rate of startups, and if they fail, they can try again. They can also connect with retired experts to solve their problems or help them find suitable partners to grow further.

- The government can also introduce certificate or diploma courses for the rural youth to train themselves to market their produce or finished products. In the coming chapters, I will list out various questions that one may ask to help them arrive at a business that is suitable for them.

Business Mindset Questions to be Asked Before Starting Business

- Why should I start a business? What are the disadvantages of the job?

- Can I pass on my job, like business, to my son or daughter? Will I continue to get the same money even after retiring from a job like business?

- Will I pay more income tax in a job or a business?

- Will I be able to motivate my children more while in a job or business?

- Will my family be more united in a job or business?

Questions to Ask Self and Information to Be Gathered While Planning to Start Business

- What are the burning needs of my surrounding area that my business can satisfy?

- What are the high-demand products that can be introduced initially to grow faster?

- How can I start a business without taking a loan?

- How can I get initial banking support if needed?

- Which raw materials can be produced by backward integration?

- Where and how can I register the products before starting the business?

- What assistance can my family members provide initially to keep the fixed costs at a minimum?

- How can the skills of those involved in the production be upgraded?

- How can one minimise waste and save energy?

- What are the resources available to me locally and at economical rates?

- What should be the initial batch size of the production, balancing the demand and requirement? Can we create our own in-house electricity-producing system by using waste, heat, or steam generated during production?

- How to get customer feedback to improve products and introduce future products?

- How soon can I start growing? How big do I want to become in six months, a year, two years, and so on?

- How can I get quality tested at a low cost initially?

- How can I advertise initially at a low cost?

- What is the profitability, and how can I calculate that initially?

- How can I get that feedback from acquaintances or the government? If the government has a PSU running in that industry, it can help from its database or database of retired experts.

- What support is the government giving to the business I am starting with regards to GST exemption initially?

- Can I get detailed information from government agencies to avoid initial teething problems or reduce them?

Contribution of Press, the IVth Estate

The press or media can limit the negative news and give more weight to the success stories of startups and entrepreneurs. If possible, there should be interviews to introduce such people and inspire others to replicate what they did.

They should also bring the success stories of women and farmers, who increased their earnings through innovation and businesses.

Part II

Introspection and Workshop

- We need to ask ourselves, depending on our strengths and ideas, which business we can start.

- Why should we start a business?

- What are our strengths and weaknesses? What business can we start according to the ideas we have?

- How can we leverage the strength of our relatives and family members to compensate for our weaknesses?

- What are the burning needs of my locality that can be converted into a business?

- Which are the high-demand products that can be introduced to grow the business faster?

- How can I do business while causing minimum waste, and making the best use of energy?

- How do I get customer feedback?

- How can I advertise initially at a low cost?

- Can I have my own in-house energy or electricity-producing system?

- How can I start with minimum capital and a minimum loan if needed?

Mentorship and Quality Control

1. Mentorship can be provided by retired food technologists, engineers, teachers, scientists, CAs, and other professionals.

2. Government quality control can help the pioneers grow with much-needed guidance.

3. JCOs and retired police officers can help them with security and discipline matters.

4. Some initial innovation support/information can be provided by scientists and scientific institutes of the state/central government. This will also provide a lot of material to students in other fields, and it will be a sort of internship for them.

Questions Regarding Mentorship from the Government

1. Is the government providing some training regarding the business or planning a visit to the nearest running business?

2. Is the government providing any online or offline facilities or apps to market the product?

3. Is the government providing information regarding the latest developments in the field of business? If so, which are the nearest government agencies and institutes?

Human Resource Development Support System

1. We must understand that once we have reached a significant level of turnover and net profit, we should give significant attention to HRD. We must understand that all the areas, from raw material procurement to processing, manufacturing, and filing of IT returns, are handled by human beings. How can we achieve success without giving HRD due importance, encouragement, and rewards?

2. We must devise a system to reward those who outperform and innovate by thinking outside the box; if extraordinary, we may even consider giving them stock options when the venture grows to that level; otherwise, more commission or some sort of partnership will be good enough. This has been mentioned because, at times, startups grow much faster, beyond our expectations, when the product is of national importance or export-worthy. These activities pay unbelievable dividends by increasing turnover, profitability, and competency.

3. We must understand that when we are ready to give, we are automatically preparing and maturing ourselves to receive more and reduce the turnout rate. This can be controlled right from the beginning when we share some incentives with the employees.

4. We must also prepare our organisation to attract the best brains and talents to work for us. The importance of HRD is understood by almost all businesspersons but is implemented by only a few. But those who are following and implementing are making a huge difference in their businesses.

Banking and Accounting Support

- Rural and urban entrepreneurs can be actively involved in cooperation with national banks to create and help captive banks. Here, I mean rural banks as subsidiaries of big banks in collaboration with farmers to address their temporary low capital needs. Here, local, educated youth can help, as they know the local population. If feasible, they can also be employed in such rural banks. This will also create employment for youth.

- A micro-entrepreneur can get the help of a local accountant for his accounting requirements.

- Law firms, retired judges, lawyers, and institutes can help entrepreneurs with legal formalities, such as getting their firms registered and applying for licences, rental agreements, partnership agreements, and other formalities.

- Retired bank officers can have their own companies where they advise entrepreneurs on how they can use the banking system for their benefit.

Questions to Ask Yourself Regarding Banking and Accounting

- Can I maintain my business account on my own? From where can I learn this? Is there some free government or subsidised training for startups?

- What type of accounting formalities are needed, if any, in the beginning? If so, which authorities should I contact?

- Is there any similar running business? The entrepreneur can consider joining an association pertaining to their business, which can be of great help.

- Is there a bank nearby where loans or loan-related subsidies are given to startups?

Questions to Be Asked or Information Gathered Regarding Finance

- How much capital is needed to start the business?

- Will it be better to start as a small cooperative or alone?

- How much of the initial cost can be kept down, and how can that grow to an appreciable level?

- Are there initial GST exemptions by the government for startups based on product/turnover, and for how long?

- In the case of government shareholdings offered, what are the extra benefits?

- In the case of potential export products, what extra facility or credit is offered by the government and the banks?

- How long would it take for the business to break even after meeting initial expenses and costs?

The above questions will help an entrepreneur manage his money well. We must also ensure that the employees are financially literate.

Product Placement Questions and Information to Be Gathered

- What is the existing size of the market, and what are the product variations available?

- How is the competitor doing his business?

- What is the information available to government agencies? If some government PSU is already doing business similar to a startup, then some of the information can be obtained from them with the help of government intervention, and a lot of time will be saved, which can be used to get other information regarding the particular startup.

- What are the product substitutes available on the market?

- Is there any availability of competitor products from government outlets? At what price are they sold?

- What are the shortcomings of the existing competitors' products?

- Is there any more scope of profit possible through backward integration or support by the government?

- How can I ensure that my product is par excellence?

Product R&D and Testing

- Is there any R&D facility available from government institutes?

- Are there quality testing and certifications available from the government or its agencies? Is there government support or training available for testing?

- Once a business picks up well, the government should help have its own R&D and quality testing lab if necessary.

Distribution

- How is the product currently distributed?

- What are the various methods of distribution, keeping in mind the cost and time taken to reach customers?

- Can we have an initial competitive edge in packing to minimise losses in transit while maintaining the quality of the product?

- What is the scope of online and offline distribution?

- Should we have our own distribution or use third-party distributors?

- We must also keep monitoring how the products are being distributed, depending on the latest distribution system. If it is old, can it be replaced by a new, cost-effective distribution system? In the later stages, we can also figure out whether the products distributed through superstores or the old distribution system are cost-effective and efficient.

- We must monitor whether monthly active users are increasing. If not, what measures should we take to increase the number of customers?

Cost Reduction Measures

- How can raw materials be obtained from the nearest place with the best cost-effective transport?

- If possible, after a few years, can a raw material supplier be involved as a shareholder or partner to increase the scale and volume of the business?

- In what volumes can the raw material be brought in to make it cost-effective?

Idea to Business Conversion

Example I

Starting a catering service

Problem: Lack of good-quality home-cooked food for people staying away from home

1. Start with identifying whom to serve and which meal to serve.

2. Prepare the food and get the target audience to try it. Get their feedback on the taste, quantity, what price they are willing to pay, etc.

3. Take orders to provide food for office-goers and small events.

4. Research on places to source raw materials from keeping in mind quality and the cost.

5. Market your products and get more orders from offices, small events, etc.

6. Once the order quantity reaches a certain level, start planning for a bigger place, hiring more staff to help, buying equipment for easy preparation, investing in your own transport vehicles, etc.

7. Consider hiring a manager to manage the operations.

8. Parallelly, start working on getting the necessary licences and look for people to help with accounts.

Example II

Readymade Garment Factory

Problem: Getting clothes stitched is becoming obsolete; everybody is going for ready-made clothes. Most of the time, it is difficult to get clothes in your own size.

- One can start with the alteration of ready-made clothes.

- As business improves through word of mouth, more sewing machines and people can be added to the team.

- One can also try getting uniform orders from companies or schools.

- The future expansion path would be to get orders from retail companies and make it into a commercial clothing manufacturing company.

The idea is to start a business using your skills. Many problems are being faced by a community. One can see it as a business opportunity and provide solutions for it. Examples would be providing accommodation for PGs; making pickles, snacks, etc., and selling them; setting up an electronic repair shop; as a real estate agent helping people find a suitable house or office space; making a team of plumbers, electricians, and carpenters to address small repair issues in the houses, offices, shops, etc.; helping students learn various subjects by taking tuition; and many more.

Analysis to make strategic changes to grow and increase profitability

We must constantly upgrade the services we provide to increase competence, competitiveness, and productivity, speed up the product's market reach, and cut down costs by asking these questions:

- How can we advertise economically?

- How can we reduce the production cost?

- Which is the best way to distribute the product?

- How can we get customer feedback faster?

- What changes are competitors making to make the product or service better?

- Which new products can be added without increasing the cost of production?

- How do I increase bulk orders?

- How do I ensure a good profit while offering competitive prices?

- We must update and upgrade the products and services. Therefore, we must keep a close watch on what the competitors and people from similar industries are offering. We must also be innovative and stay ahead of the competition.

- We must track how the product is being manufactured and finally delivered to the customers. This will help us find the loopholes and gaps occurring in between and take remedial action at the earliest.

- How do I best balance the quantity of production, storage, and supplies, effectively ensuring the products are not over or under-produced?

- After business has picked up well, get the accounts audited by a CA. Keep in contact with your bank and apprise them about your business. Your bank can help you with a loan if needed.

- We should join business associations pertaining to our business. This will keep us updated with market trends and also help us make more informed decisions pertaining to our business. We should use local resources to grow the local economy, bring down costs, and increase the number of jobs. We should also use the local speciality and convert that into a product with forward integration. We must calculate how much time is taken from raw material procurement to production and finally to reaching the customer. Where are the bottlenecks? How can we reduce this customer reach time?

In essence, we must always analyse every aspect of the business, from raw material procurement—quality, price, source, and transportation of the raw material—to manufacturing/processing, which includes ensuring that the quantity of the products manufactured is not too much or too less, uniform quality is maintained at all times, and delivery of the product, where we must ensure the product reaches on time without being damaged. All the while keeping track of finances in terms of costs incurred, salaries paid, profits earned, loan repayment, etc.

Part III

Introspection and Workshop

- How can I get mentorship from my locality or the government? Is there anyone known to do that for me?

- Does my product need R&D support?

- Should I start a service-oriented or product-oriented business?

- How can I have banking and accounting support if needed?

- How will I place my product depending on the competitor products available?

- How will I distribute my product after observing the current distribution pattern?

- How can I get customer feedback, expand, manufacture, and store the product to give it an edge compared to the competitors? Will analysing business from time to time help me to bring costs down, give better customer service, increase profitability, and grow faster?

Education System and Changes Required

The education system needs to change from being job-centric to becoming business-centric. The whole system needs to be vibrant and connect with changes taking place in the way businesses are being done.

- We can teach adults the basics, such as writing, reading, and accounting. It will help them run their business.

- Business can be taught right from the fifth or sixth grade on a part-time basis, and small businesses must be supported and guided at the school level. We can continue teaching entrepreneurship up to PhD level.

- We can invite experts from businesses and the industrial community to help people understand the changing needs of businesses in changing times.

- Courses can be added to the existing education system to help students learn and equip themselves to match up to current business environments. It can be done by providing courses on a short-term basis to help existing students think outside the box and start their own businesses. The institution can invite businessmen to conduct workshops.

- There can be practical classes to teach the students about some of the businesses, which can be done on a part-time basis. This will help low-income group or middle-income group families to rise. This can help them become self-sufficient. This will reduce the school's dropout rate and prevent child labour. This will also reduce abject poverty and juvenile crimes.

- In girls' schools and colleges, they can be introduced to businesses like starting boutiques, making pickles, jams/sauces, as well as food from home. It can help multiply family income.

- The students can also be taught to have their mini plant nurseries at home to raise the saplings of vegetables, fruits, and flowers.

- Schools can jointly fund small businesses under government supervision. This will make the education system more vibrant, lively, practical, and self-sufficient. This can be done in rural as well as urban areas.

- The curriculum in schools and colleges needs a sea change because most of what is taught is not used in practical life. The students should be given a basic knowledge of different subjects to create a strong foundation, after which they can specialise in the field of their choice.

- Once a week, senior students should be encouraged to teach junior classes under the supervision of the teachers. This will train them to teach junior students and also compensate for the absence of the teachers when it happens. This training will help them run their own coaching classes and earn their pocket money and tuition fees.

- The students should be taught the art of making notebooks for the school to make them available at a lower cost than the market.

- Those students who are interested in having their own restaurants can be encouraged to jointly make food for the annual functions or other festivals. This will make studying more interesting, and students will gain practical knowledge.

- Becoming a good sportsperson, musician, singer, actor, artist, coach, and trainer in any field is no less than a business. They can have their own small companies where they educate the children in the field of their expertise.

- Colleges should regularly host people from the government to inform students about the facilities that the government can provide to start their businesses. This will help students plan their businesses better. The students should consider their plans or the business they want to do and choose the place of internship accordingly. There should be coordination between the government, students, business houses, and the chamber of commerce. They should continuously acquaint the students with the developments.

Change of Mindset Through Education

At the school and college level, teachers can sow the seeds of entrepreneurship among the students. They must be told and reminded again and again that if they study and learn, they can be good businessmen. They can support their families and society. They can be job-givers instead of job-seekers. Students can choose their preference—to do a job or start a business. We must create more job givers, than job seekers through our education system.

Schools and colleges must encourage visits by businessmen and entrepreneurs as mentors and teachers to grow the seeds of entrepreneurship among the students and create startups.

Long-Term Impact of Entrepreneurship

- Through local entrepreneurship, the requirements of an area are satisfied locally, which saves a great deal of time and travel and provides job opportunities to people living in that area. It helps improve the economy and the standard of living.

- With interdependence on one another, there will be third-eye surveillance to check and prevent crimes. Due to coordination with the people on account of business activities, people are monitoring and keeping a close watch on the activities of suspicious characters settling in the neighbourhood. This check becomes naturally active and, therefore, is named third-eye surveillance.

- Overcrowding in cities will be reduced with the availability of opportunities locally. This will reduce great expenditure on infrastructure for an ever-increasing population in cities, resulting in national savings.

- Knowledge of retired experts like doctors, scientists, CAs, businessmen, teachers, etc., will be utilised as mentors for society, making many retired people's homes irrelevant.

- Many entrepreneurs will grow their businesses multi-fold, providing growth to the economy.

- With GDP increasing at the micro level, there will be growth in the national GDP, and we can have reduced inflation.

- An increase in business activities will also increase revenues for the government through GST and income tax.

- Sectors such as banking, logistics, marketing, packaging, and advertising services will also grow, creating more jobs.

- With more prosperity, there will be a reduction in social and economic crimes and less pressure on the courts.

- There will be fewer accidents due to limited travel. People will save fuel and time.

- Due to the growth in mindset and business, there will be need-based urban-rural connections between the companies. It can be professional synergy regarding raw material availability, better processes, technology, or market reach for mutual benefits. They can also learn from one another and take their business to the next level of growth or turnover.

- There will be maintenance of ecological balance due to local disposal of waste. The entrepreneurs will inspire their friends, relatives, and other people in society to have a business of their own.

- Many household consumables, which were not available to a section of society earlier because of their prices, will now be available due to increased business activities by micro-entrepreneurs. With this increased production, there will be more work available for manual labour as well.

- Micro-entrepreneurship may look insignificant in the beginning but will have a powerful macro-impact on the economy of a country.

- As more people get into business, more children will get exposed to business and get a chance to earn their pocket money. They will get first-hand experience of how a business works. It will also prepare them for their future endeavours.

- The children of businessmen get first-hand in-house trial and experimentation platforms to explore and experiment with new products or processes for the benefit of the business. This will lead to diversifying into new fields and the creation of new companies.

- There will also be a compounding impact of entrepreneurship on the masses, raw material producers, logistics, and services, with an increase in the volume of the business and an improved turnover YoY.

- Due to improvements in the standard of living, there will be an increase in the realisation of the value of education. People will understand the concept of small families. Not only this, but because of better living standards, there will be an increase in the number of working hours, reducing leave due to sickness.

- With better nutritional status due to an increase in income, there will be a fall in the diseases caused due to malnutrition.

- With some extra funds at disposal, there will be more demand for vehicles, clothes, and other lifestyle products. Tourism will also increase.

- Service industries like banking, insurance, legal firms, educational institutions, hotels, and the entertainment industry will also grow.

Short-Term Impact of Entrepreneurship

- Depending on the businesses people choose, many women will be empowered financially. This will reduce domestic abuse, and children will live in better environments. Women can also start their own food businesses, boutiques, or businesses in any other domain.

- Migration from villages and smaller towns to cities will be reduced.

- People will buy products locally and will find employment in their own towns and villages.

- The standard of living will improve with an increase in family income. People will be able to afford three square meals a day.

- There will be an increase in confidence, which will encourage them to take their businesses to the next level.

- Due to the overall improvement in living conditions, there will be reduced medical expenses.

- A sense of belongingness to one's own village, town, and family will increase. So there will be an increase in community service. Connecting nearby villages to cities and vice versa will lead to an exchange of knowledge, education, and economic activities, empowering one another.

- There will be more interaction with parents and grandparents. Families will become value-driven, and there will be a reduction in elder homes.

- Small businesses will start cropping up, such as fruits and vegetables, tea and snacks, etc.

Recycling of Waste

For a healthy life, we need to recycle food waste, industrial waste, and other waste to prevent water, air, and soil from getting polluted. The following measures can be useful:

- Treating vegetable waste at the household or cluster level and converting that to fertiliser.

- Convert recyclable waste into a usable form.

- Treat toxic industrial waste at industrial levels to prevent pollution of rivers and the sea and to protect marine life.

- The flowers used by temples can be reused to make incense sticks.

Some of the Challenges and Benefits in the Initial Stages of Business

As we enter the business environment, we are exposed to other businesses that are connected to ours. We interact with other businessmen and learn from their experiences and stories of triumphs and failures. We learn many unlearnt fundamentals of business practically. This prepares us to deal with the challenges our business poses. We can measure and understand the feasibility of the business in the latest business environment and its potential.

When we start a business, it connects us to similar people and companies, building a competitive edge in an ever-changing and evolving market. There is some risk in business, but our lives are always at risk at every moment. No other risk is more worthwhile than the risk of success.

Business also makes us innovative. Very often, what we see as problems will lead us to innovate and design new products or processes. We are forced to challenge ourselves, and most of the time we will be surprised by the solution we have devised. The more we face challenges, the wiser, skilled, and efficient we become.

Someone has rightly said that 'Smart brains hire intelligent brains to grow their business'.

A business takes five years on average to become profitable. We must be prepared to face the challenges that come with it, just as we have prepared ourselves to get a job and the challenges that a job poses.

In this era of interdependence, we must learn to leverage other minds to make up for our weaknesses and become more effective. We learn more by doing business than by theoretically learning about doing business. In the process, we create our own niche, goals, and plans.

Business grows our mindset and clarity to compete. It is like a practical, vibrant university where we get to learn more and earn more regularly. We elevate ourselves to invent our own decision-making capacity. We learn to handle money in a more productive and compounding way to grow more opportunities for our businesses.

A successful business can become generational, and the coming generations don't have to search for a job; they can grow and expand the existing business further.

Just as fertilisers can be made from biowaste, there is always an opportunity in the worst challenges. We learn to convert the problem into a solution that can become a business entity.

Learning the magic of treating a specific problem as a new idea provider and turning that into business is the rule of the game, which can become a daily routine. Our business helps us to review resources with feasibility, profitability, and scalability, along with a competitive edge, to grow the business to the next level.

Business in the Financial Sector

The financial market plays a significant role in the growth of the world economy because it provides the platform for individuals, businesses, and governments to invest, borrow, and raise capital. Therefore, the financial sector provides an opportunity for huge businesses and employment.

Most people in the world need financial solutions at every stage of their lives, right from childhood to retirement. One needs different financial products at every stage of their life.

The financial sector is one of the highest-paid industries in the world. This industry has created the maximum number of millionaires. There are many financial products, but some products, especially insurance products, give renewal income every year. This industry is ever-growing, and the cost of running the business is very low. You can run the business from the comfort of your own home or the office of the financial solution provider company. You don't need any office space or a large workforce. This business is in great demand in every country.

Common Home-Based Business

Possibilities in Kenya and East Africa

Businesses like home tuition, food, beauty parlours, freelance photography, etc. can be done from home. These are subject to the rules and regulations of the land, and one must procure the necessary licences before starting the business.

Possibilities of Starting Various Businesses from Home in the USA

Businesses like selling products online, writing, online teaching, consulting services, teaching yoga, real estate, home bakery, etc., can be done from home. These are subject to the rules and regulations of the land, and one must procure the necessary licences before starting the business.

Low-cost Businesses that are Possible in Canada

The following businesses can be started in Canada that require very little investment and can be started from the comfort of one's house:

- Many people don't have their own cars; people who do have cars can share a ride with them to commute to work.

- Home-cooked food businesses can be started for lunch or festive occasions, gatherings, and parties. This can be combined with other similar business entities to provide variety and choice.

- Manufacturing of jams, pickles, cakes, ketchup, pastries, etc., can be started from home.

- In Canada, almost all clothes are ready-made and are sometimes ill-fitted; ladies can have their own business from home to alter them to the required fit and charge for that.

- All businesses are subject to the rules and regulations of the land, and one must procure the necessary licences before starting the business.

Low-Cost Businesses that are possible in India

The following businesses can be done from home with little investment:

- Providing home-cooked food for offices, parties, occasions, and functions. Lunches can also be provided to schools.

- Making paper bags.

- Sewing clothes for men and women.

- Making pickles, jams, cakes, sauces, pastries, etc.

- Providing coaching classes for the students.

- Delivering groceries and items of everyday necessity to the houses.

- Providing garlands and pooja material for festivals and marriages.

- Business to provide transport facilities to school-going children and office commuters.

- Creche facility for small children of office-going parents.

- Financial services business to customers, which is highly paid and least capital intensive.

- Creating apps to connect students with teachers for coaching, doctors to patients, ambulances to patients, and customers to grocers.

These businesses are subject to the rules and regulations of the land, and one must procure licences for the businesses if required.

Home-Based Businesses to Start in Japan

Businesses in food, daycare, marketing, travel, car rentals, language learning, etc.

These businesses are subject to the rules and regulations of the land, and one must procure licences for the businesses if required.

Home-Based Businesses to Start in Dubai

The following are the businesses that can be done from home in Dubai: content writing, daycare services, tourism, real estate, content writing, cleaning services, recruitment, event management, online trade, etc.

These businesses are subject to the rules and regulations of the land, and one must procure licences for the businesses if required.

Part IV

Introspection and Workshop

- Do you want to do business in the financial sector, service sector, or products?

- Do you live in a city or village? Which businesses are popular there? Do you have some new ideas of your own?

- What are the burning mass problems that you feel can be converted into a business?

- What help do you need to learn that? Is it required for you to sign up for any course to be able to do that business?

- Which business do your friends want to do? Are some of your friends ready to become your business partners?

Conclusion

We are currently in an era where practical knowledge plays a pivotal role in transforming ideas into wealth. This transformation occurs through business connectivity, leveraging a wide range of techniques, expert insights, and a host of applications. These combined efforts propel us towards a future that surpasses our wildest imaginations.

By the time you finish reading this book, I am sure you will have realised that starting a business is not as difficult as we think. Let us decide to do it. Moreover, many businesses don't compel you to take a loan and can easily be started. We just need to align our thinking with a business mindset and initiate the business. When in a job, you connect with a limited number of like-minded people, which limits your growth, whereas a business connects you with a community. You broaden your thoughts and stretch your mindset to make your growth infinite and broaden your influence. Tata Group and Microsoft are living examples.

In the end, our business teaches us to compete with ourselves. We learn to focus on our strengths and leverage the strengths of people with the best skills and business mindsets. We further grow to evolve and find our own USP and competency. Our business keeps growing in unison with the changing society and business environment. In fact, when our business grows, it grows us both internally and externally.

Most of us come from a job mindset. Mental blocks are a part of us; they have been sown into our minds generation after generation. That is the reason we need to connect with businesspeople, which can bring about a mental shift from a job mindset to a business mindset. This shift takes time and creates some initial problems. Once your business is established, you can make an indelible mark on society and the nation at large. In a nutshell, you become a contributor to developing the economy at the national level and inspire many minds.

The business scenario in the whole world is fast changing. In the beginning, agriculture, weaving, and utensil-making were the main businesses. The population was smaller, demand was limited and there was little or no competition. What was produced was readily consumed.

As the population grew, manufacturing became mechanised with machinery. Then came accountants, distributors, lawyers, doctors, etc. With the spread of population over a large area and the availability of technology, we can use apps of different types to connect with customers and raw material providers.

We must understand that whenever there is any problem, there is a solution as well. The professional approach to solving that problem is to make a business out of the solution. COVID-19 made video conferencing and work-from-home common. This brought about a shift in the way we do business. The new way of doing business is saving a lot of money as well as time.

Manufacturing businesses were dependent on distributors for their sales. Now they can sell through many options, including need-based distribution platforms and even apps.

When we are in business, we learn every day by hearing, seeing, and experiencing. It never stops. We are the children of God, and creativity, therefore, is in our DNA. Let us take a quantum leap into the future by creating wealth through business for our generations, our nation, and for the benefit of the whole world. Let us do it this month, today, and now.

We educate ourselves to create a job mindset in us. After doing a job for a good number of years, our mindset is fixed. People all around us also add to the fixed mindset by instilling the fear that business is risky.

When we think we are ready, we must take that leap of faith. It does not take more than five years for a business to start making a profit, unlike a job. Whether in a job or a business, practical learning matters the most. There is no stability in a job unlike a business, which stabilises in five years. Doing business is more of a mindset than a skillset, which can be acquired. I am sure that by now you will have decided to start your own business.

We notice most of the businessmen around the world are not highly qualified academically. The reason is that academic education in schools and colleges provides theoretical knowledge. Ultimately, it is practical knowledge that is necessary. Every day we need to learn new things and increase our knowledge because what we learnt at school or college several years ago will not help us with our jobs or businesses in the current scenario. To remain in a job or business, we need to keep updating our knowledge with the changing environment. Just as the food we eat today may not be suitable for tomorrow, the knowledge we acquire today may not be relevant for tomorrow.

We must keep learning and updating our knowledge to stay ahead; this fact is very well understood by business people. This is the reason they hire the best minds to make themselves and their coming generations wealthy.

While doing business, we must keep the local community in mind: how can we involve them to solve the local problems and simultaneously create business opportunities for us? How can we work in the community to increase our presence and visibility?

Dreams of building a big business empire are very exciting, inspiring, and exhilarating. Let us give it wings to fly high.

If we choose a path and are determined to succeed, whatever challenges we may encounter, we can create assets and wealth that will be extraordinary. Let us give wings to our journey of entrepreneurship.

With special attention to women micro-entrepreneurs, the growth will become more inclusive in volume and uniformity. Giving special emphasis to women and agriculture is very important for economic growth and prosperity.

Our mindset, clarity, focus, determination, and confidence grow as we grow in business, which helps fuel our onward journey from one success to another.

We must understand that there are no failures; there are experiences and learnings that will help us succeed. I am sure this book will inspire some people to make up their minds to restart their long-forgotten 'traditional businesses'.

Remember, in a job, you work for money for yourself and the family, but business creates a permanent source of income and a legacy for coming generations as well. It is your choice to take up a job or start your business.

The journey to business or entrepreneurship is breathtaking! You connect with different types of people; you know society inside out; you become more humane, proactive, and sensitive to society. It changes you and transforms you to the next level by broadening your outlook as well. You become a responsible, confident, and multi-skilled human being who understands society better.

With more startups and microenterprises, there is control in price rise, increasing affordability and charity while making the world a peaceful place to live in.

With more entrepreneurs in the world, people in need of charity and the government's social schemes will be drastically reduced. This will also make a portion of the population who were earlier dependent on charity and governmental schemes independent to a certain extent. They will realise what actual independence means. The disparity-based conflicts will be reduced, making an average family's life peaceful. Many mutual conflicts among countries will become irrelevant or minimised. It can also reduce the arms race as a result.

Many countries are pinning great hopes on AI, but I strongly feel that we should first tap the human potential fully and reserve AI for hazardous jobs like mining, deep-sea searching, protecting borders, detonating bombs, fire extinguishing, managing boilers, furnaces, and nuclear reactors, installing high tension wire pillars, etc.

In the end, knowledge, which is the most precious resource of a human being, instead of getting wasted or being utilised in the business of others, is utilised in our own. What a blessing it is to create a regular source of income for generations. What better compliment could it be for God's best creation on the planet Earth? What a life it would be to live a life of prosperity!

Micro-entrepreneurship is the Solution to Most of Your Problems

It creates a permanent source of income for generations. And helps you use your knowledge in the best possible way for generations. You can use your efforts, skills, time, knowledge, and ideas to create wealth. In the distant future, your future generations will start from the level you left and grow further using their knowledge. You always have a choice: enter other businesses or become an industrialist. You become a job creator as well as a problem solver for the masses. You can start at any age, irrespective of your educational qualifications, age, or financial status.

You can fulfil your dreams, become the hero of your family, and become the troubleshooter of society. On your journey to business, you get field training, which is crucial and strengthens you at every step to finally succeed.

You become a contributor to nation-building. These contributions give many short and long-term benefits to society and the nation in the long run. This builds you, makes you the master of your destiny, and gives you a special place in society. You invent and reinvent yourself, and you feel your own empowerment.

It's a journey worth taking where you give wings to your dreams and take the first inspiring flight for your future generations. You can feel the magic in the air! There is success in the air!

www.ingramcontent.com/pod-product-compliance
Lightning Source LLC
Chambersburg PA
CBHW020328180726
47991CB00019B/1064